Life As ...

Life As an Explorer with Lewis and Clark

Laura L. Sullivan

Cavendish
Square

New York

Published in 2016 by Cavendish Square Publishing, LLC
243 5th Avenue, Suite 136, New York, NY 10016

Website: cavendishsq.com

This publication represents the opinions and views of the author based on his or her personal experience, knowledge, and research.
The information in this book serves as a general guide only. The author and publisher have used their best efforts in preparing this
book and disclaim liability rising directly or indirectly from the use and application of this book.

CPSIA Compliance Information: Batch #CW16CSQ

All websites were available and accurate when this book was sent to press.

Library of Congress Cataloging-in-Publication Data

Sullivan, Laura L., 1974-
Life as an explorer with Lewis and Clark / Laura L. Sullivan.
pages cm. — (Life as...)
Includes index.
ISBN 978-1-5026-1079-9 (hardcover) ISBN 978-1-5026-1078-2 (paperback) ISBN 978-1-5026-1080-5 (ebook)
1. Lewis and Clark Expedition (1804-1806)—Juvenile literature. 2. West (U.S.)—Discovery and exploration—Juvenile literature.
I. Title.
F592.7.S85 2016
917.804'2—dc23

2015023780

Editorial Director: David McNamara
Editor: Kristen Susienka
Copy Editor: Nathan Heidelberger
Art Director: Jeffrey Talbot
Designer: Joseph Macri
Senior Production Manager: Jennifer Ryder-Talbot
Production Editor: Renni Johnson
Photo Research: J8 Media

The photographs in this book are used by permission and through the courtesy of: Everett Historical/Shutterstock.com, cover; Public
Domain/Edgar Samuel Paxson/File:Detail Lewis & Clark at Three Forks.jpg/Wikimedia Commons, 5; Everett Historical/Shutterstock.
com, 6-7; Jennifer Thermes/Getty Images, 8; Joseph Sohm/Shutterstock.com, 11; Ed Vebell/Getty Images, 13; Private Collection/
Photo © Tarker/Bridgeman Images, 14; Tom Reichner/Shutterstock.com, 16; NPS, 19; North Wind Picture Archives, 20; Jean-Erick
Pasquier/Gamma-Rapho via Getty Images, 21; Horsesoldier.com, 22; Waltham Watches/File:Waltham Boxed Naval Chronometer,
1910.jpg/Wikimedia Commons.com, 23; ClassicStock/Alamy, 24; Painting by Stanley Meltzoff, © 2015 Silverfish Press, 27.

Printed in the United States of America

Contents

Introduction

In May 1804, a group of United States Army **volunteers** traveled into the western United States for the first time. The group was called the **Corps** of Discovery. Captain Meriwether Lewis and Second Lieutenant William Clark led it. The leaders chose thirty-one explorers to join them. They picked men who were young, strong, healthy, and unmarried. Many had experience living and working in the wilderness as hunters or trackers. Later, a Native American woman named Sacagawea (sah-ka-juh-WEE-uh) joined them. Together, the explorers traveled to the Pacific Ocean. Along the way they faced many dangers, but they also made important discoveries.

Lewis and Clark got help from a Native American woman named Sacagawea.

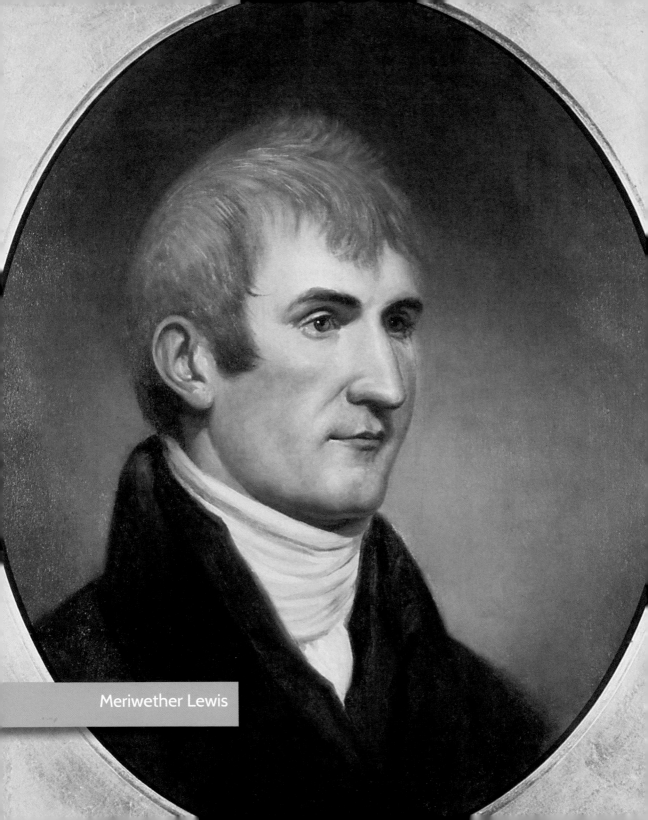

Meriwether Lewis

Chapter 1
Expanding America

Thomas Jefferson became president of the United States in 1801. He was the leader of a large and mostly unexplored country. In 1803, he bought **territory** in the West with the Louisiana Purchase. This meant the United States gained land stretching to the Rocky Mountains.

Most of that area was unexplored. The French had hunted and trapped there and traded with some of the Native American tribes, but now that the land belonged to the United States, the president needed to know

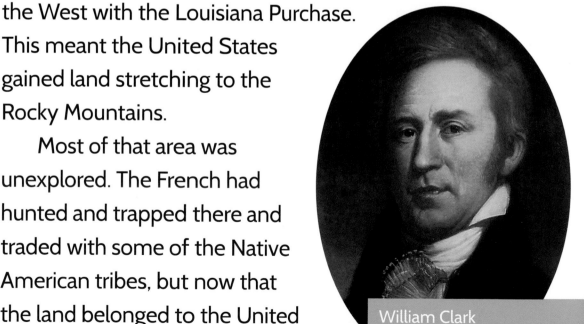

William Clark

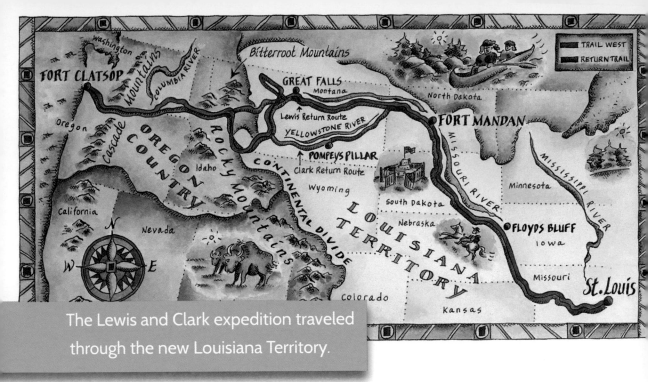

The Lewis and Clark expedition traveled through the new Louisiana Territory.

what was out there. He asked his private secretary, Meriwether Lewis, to plan a journey westward.

Lewis and his army friend William Clark led a team of hardy explorers. They were told to make friendly contact with the Native American tribes they met so the United States could trade with them. The explorers were also instructed to search for a water passage all the way to the Pacific Ocean. They hoped the Missouri River might be such a passage. Though they were wrong, they discovered many other things on their journey.

The Louisiana Purchase

In 1803, the United States bought an 828,000-square-mile (2,144,510-square-kilometer) piece of land from France known as the Louisiana Territory. It lay roughly between the Mississippi River and the Rocky Mountains. This purchase was important because it gave the United States control over New Orleans, an important port city. It also added a lot of land to the United States.

The Shoshone woman Sacagawea
helped the expedition in many ways.

Chapter 2

Joining the Adventure

Clark was put in charge of finding explorers to join him. He was looking for people used to the wilderness, able to hike for miles a day while carrying heavy supplies, and skilled at hunting. The explorers would rely on wild food such as elk, buffalo, beaver, and fish to survive.

The group was journeying into the unknown, and some of them might never return. For that reason, Clark insisted that all the explorers be unmarried. He didn't want to hurt an explorer's family if the explorer died.

Though all of the explorers were volunteers, they weren't always well behaved. Early in the trip, some drank too much alcohol, fought, or argued. Some of the men even had to be **flogged** with a whip as punishment. Later, though, order was restored and the explorers did what they had to do.

Sacagawea

Sacagawea (meaning "Bird Woman") had a difficult life. When she was twelve, her mother was killed and she was kidnapped by an enemy tribe. Later, at thirteen, she was sold to a French fur trapper, who became an interpreter for Lewis and Clark. Sacagawea joined them. She translated, gave directions, and helped them find wild food. Most important, perhaps, was simply her presence as a female. The tribes Lewis and Clark met believed they were peaceful because women never traveled with a war party.

The expedition traveled far along the Missouri River.

Ed.Velell

Scientific Training

The Corps of Discovery was on a scientific mission. Part of the explorers' training was in science. Lewis trained with four University of Pennsylvania scientists. They taught him how to preserve animal and plant samples and navigate by the stars. A doctor even gave him lessons in medicine. Unfortunately, the treatments mostly involved bloodletting and **purging**.

The river journeys could be very dangerous, with rapids, waterfalls, and grizzly bears.

Chapter 3
The Explorer's Life

Every explorer with Lewis and Clark faced extreme hardship, starvation, and danger. Many also got very sick or badly injured. Food was always a concern. Sometimes there was a lot of food, and other times there was not. When they were near buffalo herds, the explorers ate 9 pounds (4 kilograms) of buffalo meat every day. They also ate beaver tails, buffalo intestines, and dog. Other times, though, they became weak from lack of food. In one mountain snowstorm they had to eat several of their own horses. Later there were only a few dried beans and a little bear fat for each man. When they finally found a river with lots of salmon, they all cheered.

Buffalo were sometimes so plentiful that the explorers ate 9 pounds (4 kilograms) of buffalo meat daily.

Injuries were common. Men often twisted their joints or cracked their ribs. Clark's feet were severely injured by the prickly pear cactus. Lewis was accidentally shot in the buttocks by a hunter and had to travel on his belly in a canoe until he healed.

The only explorer to die on the journey was Sergeant Charles Floyd. He was twenty-two and died

A Day on the Missouri

In their trek to the Pacific Ocean the explorers hiked, climbed, rode horseback, and traveled on boats. This is what a day on the river could look like:

9 a.m.	Find shallow water, carry boats and all supplies for 2 miles (3.2 km)
12 p.m.	Lunch (leftovers)
3 p.m.	One boat capsizes when a grizzly bear attacks
5 p.m.	Stop for the night
6 p.m.	Dinner of salt pork, cornmeal, and wild game
7 p.m.	Write journal of daily observations
9 p.m.	Sleep; guards on rotating duty throughout the night

from what was probably a burst appendix. Even if he had been in a big city, doctors wouldn't have been able to save him.

Despite the dangers, there were many benefits to the explorers. They all knew that they were part of a historic mission and were seeing things their friends and family back home would never see. After the journey was over, many received bonuses for good work and got good jobs.

A monument in Sioux City, Iowa, honors Sergeant Charles Floyd, who died on the journey.

Clark drew this new bird he discovered, which he called the "Cock of the Plains."

Chapter 4
Important Supplies

Supplies for the Corps of Discovery could be a matter of life and death. The original budget for the journey was $2,500 (about $50,000 in 2015) but ended up costing $38,722 (about $800,000 in 2015). Some of that went for scientific equipment such as quadrants, compasses, a telescope, and a $250 **chronometer**. Other parts went to gifts, weapons, and food.

Though it was a peaceful mission, the explorers had to be prepared for anything. They didn't know if all of the Native American tribes they met would

Medallions like this were given to Native Americans.

The group took several kinds of rifles on their expedition.

be friendly. They also had to hunt for food. They brought many kinds of weapons. The group carried a .54 caliber rifle that had just been designed. They also had a rifle that shot a bullet using compressed air, like a modern-day BB gun. Bullets and gunpowder were also important, as were knives and hatchets.

Gifts for New Friends

One of the main goals of the journey was to make contact with Native American tribes. To help start their friendship, the Corps of Discovery brought along gifts such as sewing needles, decorative beads, colorful ribbons, fabric, and mirrors. The explorers would also trade items they used themselves, like pots, kettles, and knives. Sometimes the Native Americans gave items in exchange.

Even though they would hunt and gather food along the way, Lewis and Clark wanted to start out with as much food as possible. They brought flour, cornmeal, and salt, which could be mixed with water to make a kind of

A time-keeping device called a chronometer charted their position as they traveled.

bread. They also carried pork that had been preserved with salt. For real emergencies, they had a soup mix made of meat, eggs, and vegetables that had been boiled down to a paste. When mixed with water it made a broth.

Some of the most important supplies were also the most simple: pen, ink, and paper. Clark, Lewis, and many of the other explorers wrote down their observations as they traveled through the land. Their journals became valuable resources for historians.

Lewis and Clark did their best to befriend the Native Americans they met.

Chapter 5

The Legacy of Lewis and Clark

The explorers finally reached the Pacific Ocean in November 1805. Although they did not discover a new water route, they did create maps of the United States' new territory.

They also met many Native American tribes, including the Sioux, Shoshone, Crow, and Nez Perce. They reported on their customs and traditions and set up trade. Unfortunately, good relations with the tribes did not last. In the mid-nineteenth century, most Native Americans were forced to live on **reservations**.

The Lewis and Clark expedition involved everyone. For example, when they were deciding where to spend the winter of 1805, every member of the group got a vote, including Sacagawea and an African-American slave named York. This was long before African Americans and women could vote in the United States.

When the team returned home in 1806, they brought a wealth of knowledge about the beautiful new territory of the United States. Today the western United States continues to be a place of beauty and adventure.

No one knew if the Corps of Discovery would ever return, so there was celebration when they did.

Glossary

chronometer A device that can tell time in many harsh conditions, used along with other instruments to measure east–west distance.

corps A group of people working on the same mission; a military group assigned to a particular job.

flog To beat or whip as punishment.

purging A medical method where a doctor gives a patient a drug that causes vomiting or diarrhea.

reservation An area of land set aside for a particular Native American tribe.

territory A land or region, particularly one under the control of a specific state or government.

volunteers People who freely decide to take part in something or offer their services.

Find Out More

Books

Kitson, Jazynka. *National Geographic Readers: Sacagawea*. Readers Bios. Washington, DC: National Geographic, 2015.

Perritano, John. *The Lewis and Clark Expedition*. True Books: Westward Expansion. New York: Scholastic, 2010.

Smith, Roland. *The Captain's Dog: My Journey with the Lewis and Clark Tribe*. New York: HMH Books for Young Readers, 2008.

Website

Go West Across America With Lewis and Clark
www.nationalgeographic.com/west

Video

The Song of Sacajawea. Told by Laura Dern, with music by David Lindley. Rabbit Ears Entertainment, 1993.

Index

Page numbers in **boldface** are illustrations. Entries in **boldface** are glossary terms.

About the Author

Laura L. Sullivan is the author of more than thirty fiction and nonfiction books for children, including the fantasies *Under the Green Hill* and *Guardian of the Green Hill*. She has written many books for Cavendish Square Publishing, including *Life As a Cowboy in the American West* and *Life As a Spy in the American Revolution.*